SAVANNA
FOOD CHAINS

Bobbie Kalman & Hadley Dyer

Crabtree Publishing Company

www.crabtreebooks.com

SAVANNA FOOD CHAINS

Created by Bobbie Kalman

Dedicated by Katherine Kantor
To Peter and Nicole Szymanski and your beautiful new baby. I love you all.

Editor-in-Chief
Bobbie Kalman

Writing team
Bobbie Kalman
Hadley Dyer

Substantive editor
Kathryn Smithyman

Project editor
Michael Hodge

Editors
Molly Aloian
Robin Johnson
Kelley MacAulay
Rebecca Sjonger

Design
Katherine Kantor
Margaret Amy Salter (cover)

Production coordinator
Heather Fitzpatrick

Photo research
Crystal Foxton

Consultant
Patricia Loesche, Ph.D., Animal Behavior Program,
Department of Psychology, University of Washington

Illustrations
Barbara Bedell: pages 3 (bird, elephant, and giraffe), 11 (bird, rhino, grasshopper, and giraffe),
  18 (top and bottom), 23, 29 (leopard and grasshopper), 31
Katherine Kantor: pages 3 (all except bird, elephant, and giraffe), 6, 9 (plant and eland),
  10 (flower and snake), 11 (all except bird, rhino, grasshopper, and giraffe), 15, 19, 20,
  27 (all except dung beetle), 29 (all except leopard and grasshopper)
Jeannette McNaughton-Julich: page 10 (zebra)
Bonna Rouse: pages 9 (lion), 18 (middle), 27 (dung beetle)

Photographs
© J & B Photographers/Animals Animals - Earth Scenes: page 25
© Vladimir Kondrachov. Image from BigStockPhoto.com: page 12
© Karl Ammann/Corbis: page 31
iStockphoto.com: Joe McDaniel: page 13
Minden Pictures: Frans Lanting: page 14
Photo Researchers, Inc.: Mary Beth Angelo: page 19; Francois Gohier: page 5 (top)
Visuals Unlimited: Gerald & Buff Corsi: page 17 (top); Wendy Dennis: page 5 (bottom);
  Joe McDonald: page 18
Other images by Adobe Image Library, Corel, Creatas, Digital Stock,
  Digital Vision, and Photodisc

Library and Archives Canada Cataloguing in Publication
Kalman, Bobbie
  Savanna food chains / Bobbie Kalman & Hadley Dyer.

(Food chains)
ISBN-13: 978-0-7787-1952-6 (bound)
ISBN-10: 0-7787-1952-9 (bound)
ISBN-13: 978-0-7787-1998-4 (pbk.)
ISBN-10: 0-7787-1998-7 (pbk.)
  1. Savannah ecology--Juvenile literature. 2. Food chains
(Ecology)--Juvenile literature. I. Dyer, Hadley II. Title.
III. Series: Food chains

QH541.5.P7K34 2006   j577.4'816   C2006-904077-X

Library of Congress Cataloging-in-Publication Data
Kalman, Bobbie.
  Savanna food chains / Bobbie Kalman & Hadley Dyer.
    p. cm. -- (Food chains)
ISBN-13: 978-0-7787-1952-6 (rlb)
ISBN-10: 0-7787-1952-9 (rlb)
ISBN-13: 978-0-7787-1998-4 (pb)
ISBN-10: 0-7787-1998-7 (pb)
  1. Savanna ecology--Juvenile literature. I. Dyer, Hadley. II. Title. III. Series.

QH541.5.P7K35 2007
577.4'816--dc22

2006021838

Crabtree Publishing Company

www.crabtreebooks.com   1-800-387-7650

Published in Canada
Crabtree Publishing
616 Welland Ave.
St. Catharines, ON
L2M 5V6

Published in the United States
Crabtree Publishing
PMB16A
350 Fifth Ave., Suite 3308
New York, NY 10118

Published in the United Kingdom
Crabtree Publishing
White Cross Mills
High Town, Lancaster
LA1 4XS

Published in Australia
Crabtree Publishing
386 Mt. Alexander Rd.
Ascot Vale (Melbourne)
VIC 3032

Contents

What are savannas?

Savannas are large areas of land that are covered with grasses. Many savannas have only a few trees or **shrubs** scattered among the grasses. Others have many trees and shrubs growing in small groups among the grasses. Savannas with many trees or shrubs are also called **woodlands** or **shrublands**.

Some savannas do not have trees on them at all. Treeless savannas are called **plains**.

Always hot

Savannas are located near the **equator**, where the weather is hot all year. They are found in Australia, South America, Southeast Asia, and Africa. This book is about savannas in Africa.

Many kinds of plants and animals, including this lion, live in African savannas.

The wet season

Savannas have two main seasons. They have a wet season and a dry season. The wet season is summer. Summer weather is very hot and **humid**. Weather is humid when the air is damp. It gets so humid in savannas that it rains every day.

Monsoon winds

The wet season is also known as the **monsoon season**. During the wet season, strong winds called **monsoons** blow over savannas. Often, there are also heavy rains. Some areas of savannas flood during the monsoon season.

The dry season

The dry season is winter. During the dry season, the weather is cooler than it is during the wet season. Little rain falls during the dry season. As a result, **droughts** often occur. Droughts are long periods with little or no rainfall. During droughts, some bodies of water become dry.

5

Life on the savanna

Lemon grass is one type of plant that grows on savannas.

This bearded vulture uses its long wings to fly great distances in search of food and water.

Savannas are **habitats** for many **species**, or types, of plants and animals. A habitat is the natural place where plants and animals live. Savanna plants survive even when it is dry. They grow quickly during the wet season, when there is plenty of water. They have parts that store water, so they can survive during the dry season.

Savanna animals

Savanna animals have ways of surviving during the dry season. Many animals have long legs or wings. They can travel over great distances to find food and water. Other animals use sharp claws to dig underground homes where they can stay cool.

On the move

During the dry season, there is less water and food available in savannas than there is during the wet season. Many animals, such as wildebeests and zebras, **migrate** to habitats where water and food are available. These animals return to savannas in the wet season when there is water to drink and food to eat.

Living under ground

Animals such as snakes, lizards, and meerkats live in **burrows**, or underground homes. Living under ground helps keep these animals cool. When they are cool, they need little water. Frogs, turtles, and crocodiles stay cool by digging into the mud in rivers and **lagoons**. They stay in the mud until it rains.

The great migration

Many savanna animals live and migrate in **herds**, or large groups. Each year, herds of over a million wildebeests and half a million zebras migrate from the Serengeti National Park in Tanzania to the Masai Mara National Reserve in Kenya. This long journey is known as **the great migration**. The herds arrive in Kenya in August or September. They begin returning to Tanzania between November and January.

These wildebeests are migrating to the Masai Mara National Reserve.

What is a food chain?

There are many living things on Earth. Plants and animals are living things. All living things need air, water, sunlight, and food to stay alive.

Life-giving energy

Plants and animals get **energy** from food. Plants need energy to grow and to make new plants. Animals need energy so they can grow, move, breathe, and find food. Food also provides plants and animals with **nutrients**. Nutrients are substances that keep living things healthy.

This zebra gets energy and nutrients by eating plants.

Making food

Plants **produce**, or make, food using energy from the sun. They use some of the food energy and store the rest.

Eating food

Animals cannot produce food the way plants can. Animals get energy by eating other living things. Many animals eat plants. Some animals feed on plant-eating animals. Other animals eat both plants and animals. The pattern of eating and being eaten is called a **food chain**.

Energy in a food chain

All food chains begin with the sun's energy. Green plants take in the sun's energy to make food.

sun

plant

When an animal such as an eland eats a plant, it gets some of the energy that was stored in the plant.

eland

lion

When a lion eats an eland, energy is passed from the eland to the lion. The lion gets less of the sun's energy than the eland did.

An energy pyramid

A food chain has three levels. Plants make up the first level. Animals that eat plants make up the second level. Animals that eat other animals make up the third level.

Food producers

Plants, which make up the first level of a food chain, are called **primary producers**. They are the **primary**, or first, living things in a food chain, and they produce their own food.

Plant-eaters

Herbivores make up the second level of a food chain. Herbivores are animals that eat plants. They are called **primary consumers** because they are the first living things in a food chain that must **consume**, or eat, food.

Meat-eaters

Carnivores make up the third level of a food chain. Carnivores are animals that eat other animals. They are called **secondary consumers** because they are the second group of living things in a food chain that gets energy by eating.

10

The energy pyramid

This **energy pyramid** shows the flow of energy in a food chain. A pyramid is wide at the bottom and narrow at the top. The pyramid is wide at the bottom because there are many plants in a food chain. The second level of the pyramid is narrower because there are fewer herbivores than there are plants. The top level is the narrowest because there are fewer carnivores than there are herbivores in a food chain.

Food for plants

Photosynthesis is the process by which green plants make food. Green plants contain a **pigment**, or natural color, in their leaves. This pigment is called **chlorophyll**.

Chlorophyll **absorbs**, or takes in, energy from the sun. It combines the sun's energy with water and **carbon dioxide**. The food a plant makes is a type of sugar called **glucose**.

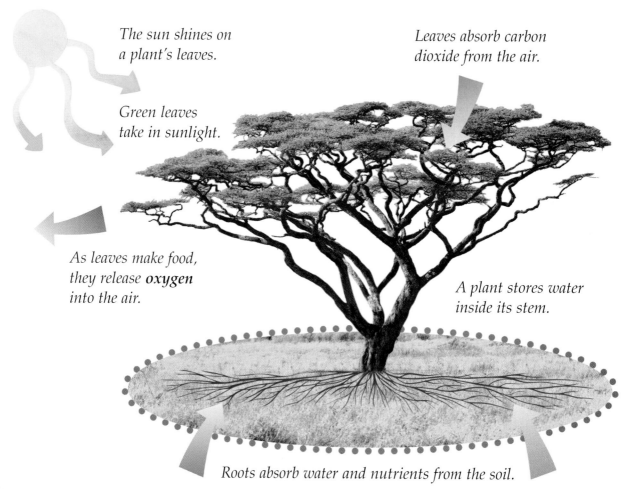

The sun shines on a plant's leaves.

Leaves absorb carbon dioxide from the air.

Green leaves take in sunlight.

As leaves make food, they release **oxygen** into the air.

A plant stores water inside its stem.

Roots absorb water and nutrients from the soil.

Plants help animals

During photosynthesis, plants absorb carbon dioxide from the air. By taking in carbon dioxide, plants help animals stay healthy. Too much carbon dioxide in the air is harmful to animals. Plants also help animals by releasing oxygen into the air. Animals need oxygen to breathe.

Designed for drought

During the dry season, many savanna plants stop making food. They stop photosynthesis to **conserve**, or save, water. The plants do not make chlorophyll, so their leaves turn from green to brown and fall off. Without leaves, the plant needs less water.

This baobab tree has dropped its leaves to conserve water during the dry season.

Savanna plants

Most savanna plants are grasses. Savanna grasses grow well in sunny, hot, and dry conditions. Some species grow to be six feet (2 m) tall! Grasses found in African savannas include red oats grass, Rhodes grass, star grass, and lemon grass.

Long roots

Savanna plants have long roots. In the dry season, these roots can reach water that is deep under the ground. Savanna grasses store water and nutrients in their roots. During the wet season, grasses grow quickly. Some grow as much as one inch (2.5 cm) in a day!

Surviving fires

During the dry season, fires start on savannas when lightning strikes the ground. Savanna grasses burn quickly, and the fires spread over large areas. The water and nutrients that are stored in the roots of the grasses keep the roots from burning, however. New grasses grow from these roots.

Savanna trees

Most types of trees need water year round. Very few species of trees grow on savannas. The dry season is too long for most species. Tree species that do grow on savannas include acacias, baobabs, commiphoras, and terminalias. Like savanna grasses, savanna trees can survive fires. Most have thick, **fire-resistant** bark. Fire-resistant bark does not burn, so it protects the trees from the flames.

Acacia defences

Most animals do not eat acacia trees. These trees have sharp thorns and branches that keep animals away. They are also tall, so their leaves are too high off the ground for most animals to reach. After an animal has eaten some acacia leaves, the tree releases a bad-tasting chemical into its other leaves. The chemical stops the animal from eating too many leaves. When one tree releases the chemical, nearby acacias also release the chemical to keep their leaves safe from the animal.

Giraffes are one of the few savanna animals that can reach the leaves at the tops of acacia trees.

15

Savanna herbivores

Wildebeests, impalas, gerenuks, elands, and these gazelles are all species of African antelopes.

There are many species of plants on savannas, so many species of herbivores also live there. Elephants, zebras, giraffes, and dozens of species of antelopes are just some of the herbivores that live on savannas. Different herbivore species eat different types of savanna plants.

Grazers

Some herbivores, such as gazelles and hippopotamuses, are **grazers**. Grazers eat grasses and other plants that grow near the ground. Each grazer species eats either a different kind of plant than those eaten by other grazers or a different part of the same plant. By eating different plant foods, many herbivores are able to graze in the same area.

A hippopotamus eats up to 80 pounds (36 kg) of grass each day!

16

Browsers

Other savanna herbivores are known as **browsers**. Browsers are animals that eat parts of bushes and trees, such as twigs and leaves. Elephants, rhinoceros, and gerenuks are browsers.

A gerenuk stands on its hind legs to reach the leaves of trees.

Savanna elephants

Elephants are **megaherbivores**. Megaherbivores are plant-eaters that weigh more than 2,200 pounds (998 kg). Elephants eat the leaves of shrubs and trees. To get the leaves, they tear off branches with their trunks or use their weight to push down trees. Elephants help new plants grow by eating seeds along with leaves. Some seeds cannot **germinate** until they pass through an animal's body and land on the ground in the animal's waste.

Savanna carnivores

Savannas are home to many carnivores, including cheetahs, pythons, and secretary birds. Most carnivores are **predators**. Predators hunt other animals for food. The animals that predators hunt are called **prey**.

Types of predators

Secondary consumers are predators that hunt and eat herbivores. Predators that hunt and eat carnivores are called **tertiary consumers**. Tertiary means "third." Tertiary consumers are the third group of animals in a food chain that eat to get energy.

An African rock python is a secondary consumer when it eats a herbivore, such as a spring hare. The python is a tertiary consumer when it eats a jackal, which is a meat-eater.

18

Population control

Predators are important to food chains. Without predators, the **populations** of many herbivores would become too large. A population is the total number of one species living in an area. For example, if cheetahs did not hunt elands, the eland population would increase, and the elands would eat too many plants. Without enough plants on savannas, herbivores would die.

The weakest links

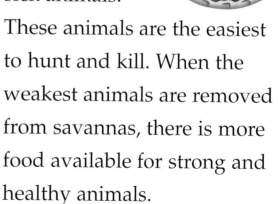

Predators often hunt young, injured, or sick animals. These animals are the easiest to hunt and kill. When the weakest animals are removed from savannas, there is more food available for strong and healthy animals.

This wildebeest may have been too slow or too weak to escape from this crocodile.

On the hunt

Predators have bodies that are suited to hunting and eating other animals. Some have sharp claws and teeth. Others have good eyesight. Most savanna predators must move quickly in order to catch their prey.

A secretary bird chases its prey and then kills it by stomping on it.

Crocodiles are hunters

Savannas are home to many Nile crocodiles. These reptiles live in water. They hunt fish as well as land animals. When animals move near the water to drink, the waiting crocodiles use their strong jaws to grab their prey. During the great migration, herds of herbivores cross rivers where crocodiles live. Lions and other predators follow the herds to hunt the animals. Crocodiles eat any animals that get too close to the water.

Catching prey

Savanna predators have many ways of catching prey. A lion creeps through tall grasses until it gets near its prey. The lion then charges toward its prey and **pounces** on it. The lion pulls its prey to the ground and kills it by biting its neck.

A bird such as an African hawk-eagle spots prey from high in the sky. The bird swoops down and uses its claws to grab the prey. African wild dogs hunt together in **packs**. They chase an animal for long distances. Once their prey is tired, the dogs attack it.

This lion has caught a zebra.

The great escape

Savanna herbivores have many predators. Herbivores have several defenses that help them stay safe from predators. There are few places to hide on savannas, so most herbivores

This kudu uses its huge horns to defend itself against predators.

are fast runners! They have large, muscular bodies that allow them to run for long distances. They also have **hooves** on their feet for running on hard ground.

Detecting danger

Good hearing and an excellent sense of smell help keep herbivores safe. These senses help herbivores detect predators from a distance. Some herbivores have **monocular vision**. Animals with monocular vision have eyes that are spaced widely apart on the sides of their heads. Widely spaced eyes allow these animals to see all around them. Being able to hear, smell, and see predators gives herbivores a chance to escape.

Safety in numbers

Many savanna herbivores stay safe by living in herds. Predators are less likely to attack a herd than they are to attack a single animal. Elands live in small herds of about 25 animals, whereas zebras live in herds of up to ten thousand animals!

Group living

By living in groups, herbivores can work together to protect their babies. When a predator is nearby, herd animals call to one another and then quickly surround their babies. The babies are safest in the middle of the herd.

Run, baby, run!

Hooved animals can walk soon after they are born. Many can even run. Being able to run allows even very young herbivores to escape predators along with their herds.

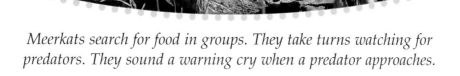

Meerkats search for food in groups. They take turns watching for predators. They sound a warning cry when a predator approaches.

Savanna omnivores

Some savanna animals are **omnivores**. Omnivores are animals that eat both plants and animals. Vervet monkeys, pigs, ratels, and ostriches are savanna omnivores.

Ostriches do not migrate. These large birds find food to eat during both the wet season and the dry season.

Vervet monkeys eat mainly fruit. They also eat insects, birds, and other small animals.

An opportunity to eat

Omnivores are **opportunistic feeders**. Opportunistic feeders eat any food they can find. Savanna omnivores eat mainly plants and seeds. They also eat insects and other small animals. Omnivores can find meals more easily than herbivores or carnivores can.

Ratels are also called "honey badgers" because their favorite food is honey. These animals also eat fruits, insects, reptiles, and birds. This ratel is digging for insects.

Keeping savannas clean

Scavengers are carnivores that do not hunt often. Scavengers eat mainly **carrion**, or dead animals. White-backed vultures are savanna scavengers. They eat only carrion. Hyenas are both predators and scavengers. They hunt prey, but they also eat carrion that other predators leave behind. Scavengers help keep savannas clean by eating the bodies of dead animals.

These white-backed vultures are eating carrion.

Breaking down

After a living thing dies, it begins to **decompose**, or break down. A decomposing plant or animal is called **detritus**. Detritus contains many nutrients. Living things that eat detritus are called **decomposers**. Decomposers get energy from the nutrients in detritus.

This dung beetle is a decomposer.

A detritus food chain

When decomposers eat detritus, they form a **detritus food chain**. In a detritus food chain, nutrients pass from detritus to decomposers and from decomposers into the soil.

Termites eat bits of dead plants to get nutrients. Their bodies use some of the nutrients. The rest of the nutrients pass through their bodies into their waste.

Note: The arrows point toward the living things that receive nutrients.

Dead plants contain nutrients.

Nutrients pass from the termite waste into the soil. The nutrients help plants grow.

A savanna food web

There are many food chains in savannas. A single food chain is made up of plants, a herbivore, and a carnivore. When an animal from one food chain eats a plant or an animal from another food chain, the food chains connect.

Two or more connecting food chains form a **food web**. Many savanna animals eat different kinds of foods. These animals belong to different food webs.

During the wet season, African wild dogs hunt grazers. In the dry season, the grazing herds migrate. African wild dogs hunt rodents and insects until the herds return.

Passing energy

This diagram shows a savanna food web. The arrows point toward the living things that are receiving food energy.

African rock pythons eat grasshoppers, spring hares, and elands.

Spring hares eat plants and grasshoppers.

Leopards eat elands, grasshoppers, and spring hares.

plants

Grasshoppers eat plants.

Elands eat plants.

Save the savannas!

Some savannas are in trouble. People destroy savannas when they use the land to grow **crops** or to feed **livestock** such as cows and goats. Livestock do not move from place to place to graze or browse like savanna herbivores do. Livestock eat the grasses in one area until all the grasses are gone. They leave no food for savanna herbivores.

Overhunting

People hunt savanna animals for food, for sport, or to protect their crops and livestock. In many areas, savanna animals are **overhunted**. Overhunting occurs when people kill too many of one animal species in an area. Overhunting harms savanna food webs. When a plant or animal species is removed from a food web, many animals are affected.

*Several savanna species, including the northern white rhinoceros, are **endangered**. Endangered animals are at risk of disappearing from Earth forever.*

Helping savannas

Many countries are helping savannas and the animals that live on them by creating **reserves**. Reserves are natural areas that are protected by governments. It is against the law to harm plants and animals on reserves. The Serengeti National Park is a reserve that protects about 5470 square miles (14,167 km²) of savanna.

Spread the word

You can help savannas by telling your friends and family about the importance of savanna plants, animals, and food webs. Discover more about savannas on the Internet or at the library.

These scientists are studying a wounded cheetah on a reserve. They will help it and then let it go.

Glossary

Note: Boldfaced words that are defined in the text may not appear in the glossary.

carbon dioxide A gas in air that plants need to make food

crops Plants grown by people for food

energy The power that living things get from food

equator An imaginary line around the center of the Earth

germinate To begin to grow

hooves Tough coverings on the feet of some animals

lagoon A small pool of water

livestock Animals raised by people for food

migrate To travel from one place to another for a period of time

oxygen A gas in air that animals need to breathe

pack A group of animals that hunts together

pounce To jump quickly to catch prey

shrub A woody plant that is smaller than a tree

Index

Printed in the U.S.A.